Ecclesia Luciferi

Lcfns
Lucifer Nostra Salus

"And no wonder, for Satan himself takes the form of an angel of light."

2 Corinthians 11:14

This satanic book is a heretical apocrypha taking the form of the Ungodly Acts of the Sect Ecclesia Luciferi.

The content of this godless book is intentionally synoptic with the oldest writings of the Nazarene sect in order to show the completely opposite theological concept - the mystery of godlessness, the only weapon that has the power to kill imaginary gods.

Ecclesia Luciferi

Before departing into eternity, Light-Bearer breathed an ungodly spirit into his followers. For many nights he tormented them in dark visions and gave them ambiguous evidence that he was in fact, as it were, undead. He spoke to them of Satan's power to control the minds and hearts of the last people. In the night visions they heard whispers: "Do not go away, but await what is to come. You will soon be possessed by an evil spirit". So when they gathered together, they asked the whisperers: "Will the kingdom of flesh and blood soon come?". They were told, "You will not comprehend it now. But when the godless inspiration enters you, you will receive knowledge and the power of the will, and you will be witnesses to The Son of Dawn in a world of superstition and delusion." They then saw, as if in a dream, a figure which, having spread its bat-like wings, floats upwards until it

finally turns into a light brighter than the sun and suddenly disappears.

While they were still covering their eyes from the blinding light, suddenly a goat on two legs stood beside them and said: "Do not be afraid or surprised at what you have seen for every one of you who accepts the teaching of the Anti-god will become a reflection of the light before he passes away into Nothingness".

Then they returned to the city. When they arrived there, they went into the attic of the house where they were staying. They all spent time there being as if in lethargy.

In those days Primus stood in the midst of those gathered and said: "Godless ones, it has happened as The Son of Dawn foresaw in the case of Teritus Decimus, who contributed to the enslavement of the Arch-Man. He was one of us and his self-will led to the events we all witnessed.

Afterwards, as you know, an unfortunate accident happened to him. He fell head down from the attic and hung from a tree,

and all his entrails came out of his torn abdomen. News of this spread among all the inhabitants of Aela Capitolina.

It is imperative, therefore, that we choose one of the ungodly who accompanied us throughout the time that Light-Bearer worked among us - from the moment he was possessed by an evil spirit until the day he departed into Nothingness - so that he can testify with us to his sinful power of transformation from death of spirit to godless life." They proposed two: Caesius, and also Spurinne. Then, in exultation and ecstasy, they began to malign heaven and cried out: "Satan, You know the hearts of men. Show us which of these two Thou hast inspired to take the place of Teritus Decimus. For he has abandoned his complicity and gone his own way towards the Abyss."

Suddenly Spurinne's face changed, took on the appearance of a corpse. And he was added to the ranks of the ungodly.

Some time later, one night they were all staying together in the old chapel. Suddenly, as if from the Abyss, a sound like the groans of the dying rang out and filled the whole room they were in.

And they saw, as it were, torches of fire which divided and set fire to each of them in turn. Then they were all filled with an evil spirit and began to roll on the ground with foam on their lips, some laughing as if possessed and others mumbling something in an incomprehensible, terrifying, demonic language.

At that time the worshippers of the god YHWH from various countries were also staying in Aela Capitolina When, therefore, the sound rang out, the flock gathered.

And they all fell into terror, for everyone heard their god being cursed in their own language. Unable to get out of their fear and amazement, they said: 'Don't all these people speak in the language of demons. How then is it that each of us

hears blasphemies in our own language? We all hear these people cursing in our tongues the faulty works of YHWH."

Indeed, everyone was so frightened and confused that they asked one another: "What can this mean?".

Then Primus stood up together with the ungodly and spoke loudly in a voice so strange that not everyone managed to listen to him: "Visitors and all the inhabitants of Aela Capitolina, listen carefully to what I am about to say. What you see has been prophesied by the possessed: '"In those days I will breathe an evil spirit upon the frightened people. And your demon-possessed sons and daughters will prophesy in sinful inspiration, the young among you will see godless visions, and the old will have dreams of eternal emptiness. In visions you will see signs in heaven and on earth - there will be blood, fire and clouds of smoke. The sun will turn to darkness and the moon to blood before nothingness comes. People, listen:

The Arch-Man was inspired by Satan. He has clearly demonstrated this through ungodly works, revealed miracles and ambiguous signs, which, as you yourselves know, he performed among you through him.

This Arch-Man was handed over to you because he himself decided so.

And you hanged him, you put him to death with the hands of hypocritical people, believing that in this way you would purify yourselves of the sin, evil and darkness that is within you. You sacrificed him as your fathers sacrificed a goat to the saviour Azazel. You have thus acknowledged that Light-Bearer is indeed the true saviour.

But your sacrifices to a vengeful god have no meaning. You will not be free until you believe that there is no original sin.

You must sacrifice your spirit to live in flesh and blood.

But the Anti-God has resurrected Him within you again, has freed you from the power of eternal punishment for

imaginary sins, for it was unthinkable that the power of evil should hold you forever in its grip.

The Knower says of him: "You have shown me the way of a strange life. When I dwell in your sinful presence, I am filled with sorrow because joy is for fools."

"People, let me tell you openly about the Knower who died and was buried and his body turned into nothingness.

He, foreseeing what was to happen, spoke of the transformation of the Arch-Man, that although he was left in the grave and his body rotted, the spirit of godlessness turned into an eternal shadow, which embraced all the self-conscious, and which became a reflection of light to those who are able to comprehend it. The Anti-god has resurrected Lucifer in us and we are all victims of this. Because the Arch-Man has been exalted into the image of Satan, he has breathed the satanic spirit upon us, as you yourselves can see and hear. Therefore, you rightly feel that

Light-Bearer, who sacrificed himself, has been set up by Satan as a mystery of ungodliness."

When they heard this, they felt as if the spirit of delusion had been killed in them, and they turned to Primus and the rest of the godless: "Blasphemers, what shall we do?". Primus said to them: "Show no remorse or guilt, and let each of you consume the blood. And then you will receive the gift of the spirit of ungodliness. In nomine Dei nostri Satanas Luciferi excelsi!

And Primus told them many other strange and disturbing things. He bore witness to their deception and continued to tempt them: "Reject this corrupt, superstitious and fearful life".

So those who wanted to, consumed blood. That night, several hundred people joined the ungodly. And the Luciferians revealed many false miracles and signs and all the godly people began to fear them. And every night they haunted the temple tempting the followers of YHWH.

They met in various houses to perform rituals, with sinful joy and with animalistic desire sharing their bodies with each other and glorifying the Anti-god. And through Satan, they were joined daily by others entering the path of liberation from sin.

On one occasion, when Primus and Quartus were going to the temple for the local hour of prayer, they happened to be carrying a man who had had unfit legs since birth. Every day he was laid down at the temple gate so that he could beg.
When he saw Primus and Quartus, who were just entering the temple, he too began to ask them for a donation. They looked at him carefully, whereupon Primus said: "Look at us". So he looked at them, expecting to get something from them. Primus, however, said: "In the name of Lucifer I say to you: 'Believe that you are innocent and that your will is power. Get up and come!"
As he took him by the right hand and lifted him up, his bones immediately

strengthened. And then he straightened up and began to walk. And he went with them into the temple and walked and hopped about, praising the Anti-god. And the people saw him walking and glorifying Satan.

When they recognised in him the man who usually sat at the temple gate, begging, they fell into great surprise and horror at what had happened to him.

The man did not depart from Primus and Quartus, and the whole people, unable to recover from their astonishment, converged on them. When Primus saw this, he spoke: "People! Why is this so surprising to you?

And why do you look upon us as if it were through our own power or our devotion to a false deity that this man began to walk?

The Anti-god inspired The Son of Dawn, whom you mocked before the priests.

Yes, you mocked the enemy of blind faith and superstition. And you killed the Herald of Ungodliness. But the Anti-God has immortalised him in us, of which we

are the witnesses. It is because of his teaching on the power of the will that this man, whom you see and know, has regained strength in his legs. His faith in himself and in the power of the Will, which we have thanks to Lucifer, caused him to recover completely before your eyes. Now I know, O slave of blind faith, that you acted in fear. But in this way the Anti-god had to immortalise The Son of Dawn. "Therefore, show no more repentance and fear, and reject faith in sin. And then, through Satan, the times of doubt will come."

As Primus and Quartus spoke to the flock, the priests approached them.

Angered that ungodly men were teaching the people and speaking openly about Luciferian transformation, they seized them, but as it was already evening, they put them under guard until the next day. However, many of those who listened to the speakers believed, and the number of accomplices increased considerably.

The next day, the leaders and priests, including the chief priest Sergius, gathered together in the Aela Capitolina. They ordered Primus and Quartus to stand in the middle and began to question them: "Where did you get such power? In whose name did you do this?". Then Primus, possessed by an evil spirit, said to them: "False rulers of the souls and minds of the godly flock and you overseers of the slaves of the faith, if we are being questioned today because of the manifestation of the power of the will on the crippled man, if you want to know who healed him, then accept the fact, all of you and all the people, that it happened through the recognition of the ungodly teaching of Light-Bearer, whom you ordered to be hanged, and whom Satan resurrected in the heart of this poor man. It is because of him that this man stands before you sane.

The fact that this man, rejecting the dogmas and superstitions of your cruel religion in which he was brought up, believed that he could save himself has

become a scandal to you. But there is no one else who can set us free. Only we ourselves, inspired by The Son of Dawn, can do it." When they saw the indifference and lack of fear of Primus and Quartus and realised that they were, after all, ordinary people, they fell into amazement. They began to realise that they were accompanying Light-Bearer.

Looking at the healed man who was standing with the godless, they did not know what to answer.

So they ordered them to leave the church hall and began to confer among themselves. They said: "What should we do with these blasphemers? After all, they have done something disturbing. The people of Aela Capitolina know about it and we cannot deny it. So let us not allow this matter to gain even more publicity among the people.

Threaten them not to speak again with invoking this forbidden name".

Then they called them and forbade them to speak and teach with invoking the name of The Son of Dawn. But Primus

and Quartus replied: "What is right - to listen to sinful whispers or to your god? Judge according to your will. We, however, do not want to stop talking about what we have seen and heard and what we have thought".
So they threatened them once more and released them, for they found no basis for punishing them. Besides, they were afraid of the flock, because they all praised Anti-god because of what had happened.

When the ungodly were released, they went to the rest of the accomplices and relayed to them the words of the chief priests and leaders of the people. After their account, they all ran amok and chaotically, shouting at each other, began to shout to Satan: "Satan it is you who have invented the illusion of free will, apparent pride, self-confidence, the spirit of rebellion and scepticism. Priests, hypocritical, frightened, jealous and greedy people have gathered in this city against the one whom you inspired,

against The Son of Dawn - that the sinful intention, what was planned, might be self-fulfilled. Deceiver, heed their threats and help the heralds of godlessness to boldly persuade this superstitious people.

And continue to use our fanaticism to deliver from imaginary sin. Let, in the name of the Arch-Man, ungodly signs and wonders happen."

When they had finished speaking, the place where they were gathered shook, and they were all inspired by an evil spirit, and began to preach ungodly doctrine with arrogance. Pride and contempt for ignorance reigned among all the great number of doubters. And no one said that what they had belonged to them, because they did not care. And the godless continued to bear witness to the Luciferic transformation with blasphemous certainty.

And they carried out many profanities among the people. Few had the courage to join them, but in general the people expressed themselves about them with

apparent respect. And those who embraced doubt continued to increase. And they carried the spiritually ill even into the main streets.

They were laid on stretchers and mats so that at least the cold shadow of a passing Primus could fall on some. People from the towns around the Aela Capitolina also came in crowds. They brought with them the sick and those plagued by the spirits of blind faith and superstition, and those who recognised the impiety healed themselves.

But the high priest and all who accompanied him, full of jealousy, rose up against the blasphemers, seized them and threw them into the dungeons.

But at midnight they had a vision; behold, a demonic figure appears and opens the dungeon, leads them out of it and says: "Go to their temple and, cursing the Usurper, teach the people about life in flesh and blood, in abundance and lack of fear". When they heard this, they entered the temple at dawn and began to

teach. Meanwhile, the high priest and his men arrived. They convened a council and sent for the ungodly to the dungeon. But the guards did not find them in the dungeon.

So they returned and said: "When we came, the dungeon was closed, and there were guards standing at the door. But when we opened it, we found no one inside." When the temple superintendent and the chief priests heard these words, confused, they began to wonder what would come of it. Then a man came and reported to them: "The people whom you have locked up in the dungeon are standing in the temple and teaching the people by cursing YHWH". So the temple superintendent and the guards went to bring in the blasphemers - but without using force, for fear that the people would kill them. When they brought them in and brought them before the council, the high priest began to question them. He said: "We have strictly forbidden you to teach in this sinful name. And what are you doing? You are

teaching throughout the city. And you want the punishment for ungodliness to fall on the people." Primus and the other godless men replied: "First of all, we cannot be disobedient to reason. The Anti-god has caused the Arch-Man to rise up in us, the Son of Dawn, whom you have hanged.

He exalted him to become one with him, and made him the Accuser of hypocrisy and the Liberator from the chains of superstition, so that the people might be godless and reject the warren into sin. And we are witnesses to this. The evil spirit, which Satan breathes into whomever he wills, also testifies to this."

When they heard this, they flew into a rage and wanted to kill the blasphemers. But a member of the council named Lar, a priest, got up from his seat and had them led away for a while. He then said: "Members of the council, think carefully about what you want to do with these people. Some time ago Titus, who thought he was someone

important, appeared and several hundred men joined him. But he was killed, and then all his followers dispersed and the trace of them disappeared. Then, Vibius appeared and gathered people around him.

But he too was killed, and all his followers dispersed. Therefore, I now advise you: leave these people alone, do not interfere in their affairs.

For if their intentions and actions are along the lines of faith a human invention, nothing will come of it, but if it comes from Satan, you will not be able to stop them. In addition, you may find that you are fighting the Anti-God."

And they heeded this advice.

They summoned the blasphemers, flogged them and forbade them to speak invoking the name of Light-Bearer, and then let them go. So they left before the council indifferent, without a shadow of fear, despising the priests and the hypocritical church. And they continued every night in the temple and after the

houses to teach and deceive constantly with the teaching of Light-Bearer.

And there was Faustus among the blasphemers, inspired by Satan, full of sinful power, performing miracles of the power of the will and signs among the people. Some of the priests began to have disputes with him. But they were unable to confront him, for in what he said, the godless wisdom and inspiration of the evil spirit was evident.
Then they said: "We heard him uttering blasphemies against Maruttash and Uzurpator." And they stirred up the flock, and the elders and the priests, and they came suddenly and forcibly seized him and took him before the Council. They brought in false witnesses who testified, "This man is constantly saying things against this holy city and against Yahweh's law. For example, we heard him say that the Arch-Man would shake up the church and reject the laws that Maruttash gave us." And all those sitting in the Council gazed at Faustus.

And they saw that his face looked like a cold boulder.

The high priest asked: "Is it true what they say?".

Faustus full of the spirit of ungodliness, looked up into the dark sky and saw in vision shadows like horned beasts in the sky. And he said: "I see the heavens open, burning, and the Fallen Angel standing over the grave of a god. I see cold emptiness and Nothingness. I see eternal freedom. There is nothing there." Then they shrieked like possessed men at full volume and all rushed at him together.

They dragged him outside the city and began to stone him in the name of their god, whom they call love. And they threw stones at Faustus, and he fell to his knees and whispered: "I am no longer afraid. I am free for ever." After these words he departed into the Void.

On that day, the great persecution of the Anti-god sect in Aela Capitolina began and all but the godless dispersed

throughout Dawn. These fearlessly burned the corpse of Faustus and paid homage to his sinful knowledge. And there was a certain man named Vicarius. He began to pasture the Sect. He broke into one house after another, dragged out both men and women and committed them to prison. Meanwhile, scattered blasphemers went across the country and spread the teachings of the Son of Dawn, preaching liberation from the chains of superstition.

One of them, Episcopus, came to the city of Assur and began to preach to the people about Lucifer.

The crowds who listened to him, and who saw what deceptions and signs he was performing, unanimously accepted his teaching. For many had been under the influence of false spirits and angels, and now these spirits were fleeing from them with a shout. Many who were paralysed and lame were healed by the power of the will, but some were not healed. There was carnal joy in the city.

And there was a man in the city named Primas, who was involved in magic and who amazed the people of Assur. He claimed to be someone powerful. And everyone reckoned with him. They said, "There is a great sacred power hidden in this man".

They reckoned with him because he had been astonishing them with his magic tricks for a long time. But when they believed Episcopus, who preached the death of the spirit and praised Lucifer's sin, they decided to consume the blood - both men and women. Primas himself also believed and, since he had been transformed, constantly accompanied Episcopus.

He was amazed to see what strange signs, what great and ungodly works he was doing. When the godless in Aela Capitolina heard that the people of Assura had accepted the teaching of the Son of Dawn, they sent Primus and Quartus to them. And they, when they arrived there, performed the ritual of the death of faith, so that the people would

receive the spirit of godlessness. Primus and Quartus began to put their hands on them and the people, falling into a rage, received the evil spirit.

Once they had given a demonstration of the power of godlessness there and recounted the word of The Son of Dawn, they set off back to Aela Capitolina and preached Lucifer's doctrine in many Dawn villages along the way. But the spirit said to Episcopus in a vision: "Go north towards the road". So Episcopus went. Just then a Kemetic official passing that way was returning home. Sitting in his chariot, he read aloud the writings of the Knower.

So the spirit said to Episcopus: "Run like a dog to that chariot".

Episcopus did so, and running on all fours beside the chariot, he heard the Kemetian reading aloud a book. He asked: "Do you understand what you are reading?". He replied: "How can I understand when no one has explained it to me?". And he begged the Episcopus to come into the chariot and sit by

him. And he read aloud this passage: "He was led like a goat into the wilderness. And in his pride he did not open his mouth if he did not want to. They tried to humiliate him and denied him a just sentence. Who exactly will tell of his origin? His life on earth was taken from him." Kemetian turned to Episcopus: "Tell me, please: Who is the knower talking about here? About himself or about someone else?".

So Episcopus, beginning with this passage of scripture, began to preach to him the ungodly teaching of Light-Bearer. As they rode along the road in this way, Episcopus departed in a vision, and the Kemetian, shocked and amazed, continued on his way. And he never saw Episcopus again.

Episcopus himself traversed the Dawn territories, preaching godless doctrine in all the cities until he reached the capital. And Vicarius was still sowing terror and burning with a lust for murder against Light-Bearer's chosen ones. He went to the high priest and asked for

authorisations for the churches in Akad, so that any blasphemers he found there - both men and women - could be brought in bonds to the Aela Capitolina.

On his journey to Akad, as he was already approaching the city, a light suddenly flashed around him. Vicarius fell to the ground, and then he heard a vicious whisper, like the hissing of a snake: 'Vicarius, Vicarius, why do you wander in the dark?' He asked: "Who are you, O Godless One?".
And the One said: "I am the Flame which thou seekest to extinguish. Arise and go into the city. There you will learn what you must do next." Those who travelled with him stood stunned, for they heard only some terrible whispering, but saw no one.
When Vicarius got up from the ground, they found that although his eyes were open, he could see nothing. So they took him by the hand and led him to Akad, and he saw nothing for six days. During that time he did not eat or drink.

In Akad was one of the godless men named Pontifex. A voice spoke to him in a delirious vision: "Pontifex!". He replied: "I am sensing." The voice whispered to him: "Get up, go to Transfiguration Street, to Marcus' house. Ask there about a man named Vicarius. He happens to be in a state of possession and saw in a chaotic vision you, Pontifex, how you came and put your hands on him so that he could regain his sight." Pontifex then replied: "I have heard of him from many people, how much harm he did to your blasphemers in Aela Capitolina. Here, too, he came with authority from the chief priests to arrest all who follow the path of the shadow." But the Voice whispered to him: "Go! For this man is my torch. He will carry my name to the superstitious nations.

I will clearly show him what suffering is for the sake of my godless name.'

So Pontifex went to that house, put his hands on Vicarius and said: "Vicarius, erring one, The Son of Dawn, who appeared to you on the way, sent me to

make you recover your sight and be filled with an evil spirit".

He then immediately regained his sight. Then he consumed blood.

Some time he remained with the ungodly in Acad. He also immediately began to preach in the churches that Light-Bearer was the Arch-Man. All who heard him were amazed and asked: "Is this not the man who fiercely persecuted the godless in Aela Capitolina? Didn't he come here to arrest them and lead them to the priests?".

And Vicarius acted with increasingly sinful power and embarrassed the priests living in Akad, as he logically proved that Light-Bearer was anti-god.

When Vicarius arrived in Aela Capitolina, he tried to make contact with the godless, but they all despised him because they did not believe that he too had become a witness to Lucifer.

Then Pontifex came to his aid. He led him to the impious and told them in detail how, on the way, Vicarius had seen Light-Bearer, how he had spoken to him,

and how later in the Acad he himself had spoken boldly with sinful power.

Vicarius therefore remained with them and moved freely around the city, boldly speaking in satanic inspiration. He also spoke and held discussions with the priests of YHWH. They, however, attempted to kill him. When the ungodly found out about this, they sent him away. Then suddenly there was a period of calm for the Sect throughout Dawn.

The blasphemers lived in contempt of the Usurper and experienced the constant influence of the evil spirit, so that their numbers grew steadily.

As Primus travelled throughout the area, he also visited the godless in Uruk. There he met a man named Judas, who was paralysed and had been immobilised in bed for six years.

Primus said to him: "Judas, if you really reject belief in original sin and believe in the power of the will, then get up and walk." And he immediately stood up. And all of Uruk and the plain of

Internum who saw him believed in the power of the Will.

In Ur there lived a girl named Laris. But just in those days she fell ill and died. So she was washed and laid in the attic. Since Uruk was close to Ur, the ungodly, who heard that Primus was in that city, sent two men to summon him: 'Come at once!' Primus went with them. When he arrived and they ushered him into the attic, Primus ushered everyone out, raised his dead gaze to the sky and uttered some incantations in a strange language. He then turned his countenance, which had assumed a terrifying, grotesque appearance, towards the body and whispered: "Laris, you are undead. To you I say wake up!" Then she opened her eyes and at the sight of Primus she screamed.

He gave her a hand and helped her up, after which he called out to the godless, including the women, and they all saw her undead.

News of this spread throughout Ur and many believed in Lucifer's name and the power of Knowledge.

And Primus remained in Ur for a long time. He lived in the gravedigger's house.

In the Internum lived a man named Mamertis, a soldier of the legio. On one occasion, somewhere around 6 o'clock, he clearly saw in a vision a demon who came to him and said: "Mamertis!". Mamertis looked at him and, frightened, asked: "What is it?". And he replied: "Send men to Ur to fetch a man named Primus, called Denial.

He is hosted there by an undertaker who has a house in the cemetery'. When the demon left, Mamertis immediately summoned three of his slaves. He told them everything and sent them to Ur. The next day, when they were already approaching the city, Primus had just entered the cellar of the house to fall into lethargy. It was then about 6 p.m. However, he was very hungry and

wanted something to eat. While his food was being prepared, he received a vision.

He saw an open black sky and something like a large dark sheet being lowered to the ground by its four ends. On it were animals already dead and bloated. Then he heard a kind of disturbing whisper: "Get up, Primus, and eat!". To this he said: "Oh no! I have never eaten carrion." Then he heard the disturbing voice a second time: "They are already carrion when they are alive. They are dead. They are dead. Their truths stink like carrion. The day will come when we will devour them and expel them." When he heard it for the third time, all the filth was immediately taken to the abyss. Just then the men sent by Mamertis, who had already managed to find out where the gravedigger's house was, stood in front of the gate. They loudly asked if Primus was hosted there.

As Primus contemplated this strange vision, the spirit said to him: "Three men are looking for you.

Go down, then, and go with them without hesitation, for it was I who sent them." Then Primus went down to these men and said: "It is I you seek. What brings you here?" They said: "We were sent by the legionary Mamertis.
The Spirit commanded him to summon you to his house and listen to what you have to say." So Primus invited them in and hosted them. The next day he rose and set out with them, accompanied by some ungodly people from Ur.

The next day he reached the Internum. Mamertis was already awaiting them.
As Primus entered the house, Mamertis came out to meet him, fell to his feet and paid him homage. But Primus lifted him up, saying: "Get up you fool. Do not fall to your knees before anyone. Be proud!". Speaking to him, he went inside and found many gathered there. He said to them: "You know well that the followers of YHWH are not allowed to approach a man from another nation or to have close relations with

him. But I despise their laws and know that no man should be called defiled or unclean. Therefore, when I was sent for, I came without hesitation. So tell me why you have brought me". Then Mamertis said: "Four days ago, at this very time, at 6 o'clock, when I experienced a vision in my house, a man in a black robe stood before me and said: 'Mamertis, send men to Ur for a Primus called Denial. He is staying in the gravedigger's house, in the graveyard. Therefore I sent for you at once, and you agreed to come here.

So we are all assembled here in the face of the Anti-god to hear all that you have to say." Then Primus spoke: "Satan is indifferent. His attention can be expected by everyone. He has inspired some people with his teaching of liberation from superstition, from belief in a god from the desert, from fear of punishment for the lie of original sin. You know what was spoken of throughout Dawn, and what began after the possession of the evil spirit that the

Knower preached about. Light-Bearer was spoken of, how the Anti-God inspired him with a spirit of godlessness and bestowed upon him sinful knowledge, and he went about the land, did what he wished, and raised him to life in flesh and blood. We are witnesses to all that he accomplished both in Aela Capitolina and throughout this superstitious country.

However, they hanged him and killed him. But the Anti-god resurrected him in the cold hearts of the godless, who rejected the offer of the false god and eternity in fear of his wrath. After the death of the spirit and the rebirth of the flesh occurred, we indulged in animal joy in flesh and blood knowing that tomorrow we would die.

We found it necessary to preach to the flock and testify that he was the Arch-Man.

All thinkers of godlessness attest that anyone who does not believe in the gods, according to his teaching, accesses freedom in sin."

While Primus was still speaking, an evil spirit inspired all who heard this. They began to laugh hysterically, some rolled foam from their mouths and cursed the name of YHWH, and others began to speak in demonic language and exalt Satan. Then Primus said: "To those who, like us, have received an evil spirit, can anyone refuse to eat blood?".

The blasphemers in Dawn heard that people from other nations had also succumbed to ungodliness.
So when Primus came to Aela Capitolina, the proponents of ritual mutilation began to criticise him. They said, "You went to the house of unmutilated people and ate with them".
Then Primus began to explain the matter to them in detail: "When I was in Ur and fell into lethargy, I saw in a vision something like a dark sheet being lowered from the sky by its four ends. It stopped right next to me. When I looked closer,

I saw all sorts of dead and decayed animals on it. I also heard a kind of disturbing voice: 'Get up, Primus, and eat!' To this I said: 'Oh no! I have never eaten carrion'. Then I heard a strange voice a second time: 'They are already carrion when alive. They are dead. They are dead. Their truths stink like carrion. The day will come when we will devour them and expel them'. When I heard it for the third time, everything was pulled back into the abyss. At that exact moment, three men sent to me from the Internum stood in front of the house we were in.

Then the spirit of the disturbing visions told me to go with them without hesitation.

The six ungodly men also set out with me and we came to the man's house. "He told us that he saw a demon appear in his house and said: 'Send men to Ur for a Primus called Denial, and he will tell you by which you and your whole house can be rid of illusions.' When I spoke, they were inspired by an evil spirit, just as we

were in the beginning. If, then, the Anti-God has given them the same gift as to us who have rejected Yahweh, who am I to get in his way'. When the ungodly heard this, they stopped making objections. They said: "So Satan has also shown to the people of other nations the power of doctrine which leads to abundant life".

And the blasphemers, who had dispersed as a result of the persecution after the death of Faustus, reached as far as Sippar, Kish and to Isin.
The power of godlessness was with them and a multitude of people understood and rejected religious superstition and the worship of a false god. When news of them reached the sect in Aela Capitolina, Pontifex was sent to Isin. And he, when he arrived there and saw the manifestations of pride, knowledge and scepticism, rejoiced and began to encourage them all to resolve with all their hearts to believe in themselves and in the power of the Will.

For he was a cunning man, strong-willed and full of a spirit of rebellion. And many people believed in Lucifer.

Then Pontifex went to find Vicarius.

When he found him, he brought him to Isin. For a whole year they met together with the local Sect and deceived a large crowd of people. And for the first time it was in Issin that the godless were called Ecclesia Luciferi.

It was around this time that King Urbanus began to persecute some members of the Sect. Teritus, the brother of Quartus, had him beheaded with an axe. When he saw that this pleased the priests, he also decided to arrest Primus. He captured him, threw him into a dungeon and put him under the guard of the soldiers. After their feast, he intended to hand him over to the flock.

So Primus was kept in the dungeon. During the night - just before Urbanus was about to hand him over to the flock - Primus fell into lethargy

between two soldiers, chained together. The guards also stood outside the entrance.

Suddenly, a light seemed to flare up in the cell and someone resembling neither man nor animal appeared. It seemed to speak to Primus, saying despite not moving its snout: "Do what I tell you!".

At that moment he felt as if the chains had fallen from his hands. The figure then said to him: "Follow me". So he stepped out of the cell and followed him, but he did not know if what was happening through the phantom was really happening. Rather, he thought he was having a vision. When they passed the first and second guards and reached the iron gate facing the city, the gate itself opened. So they went outside, walked down one of the streets and the phantom suddenly disappeared Then Primus realised that dark dreams could also be reality. When he realised this, he went to the house where the Sect was gathering.

He knocked on the gate door and then one of the women came out. When she recognised Primus' voice she ran back inside and said that Primus was standing in front of the gate.

They said: "This is his reflection".

Meanwhile, Primus continued to stand there and knock. When they opened the door and saw him, they were astonished. And he gave them a sign with his hand to be silent, and told them in detail how in a vision the phantom had led him out of the dungeon. Then he said: "Inform the ungodly of this."

Then he left there and went elsewhere. When daylight came, the soldiers, not knowing what had happened to Primus, fell into a great panic. Urbanus launched a search but did not find him.

So he questioned the guards and had them flogged. And he himself set off from Dawn to the Internum and spent some time there.

On the appointed day Urbanus dressed himself in a priestly robe, sat down in

the magistrate's chair and spoke to them. Then the assembled people began to exclaim: "This is the voice of a god, not of a man!". Then Urbanus suddenly collapsed. And he died, eaten by vermin.

And the godlessness continued to spread and the development continued.
Pontifex and Vicarius, once they had done their work elsewhere, returned to Isin.
In Isin they were in the local sect of the knowers. When they happened to be performing rituals, an evil spirit inspired them to say: "Separate Pontifex and Vicarius for me, so that they can spread the plague of godlessness". Then they laid hands on them and set them on their way. So they, inspired by an evil spirit, arrived in Kish and began to preach The Light-Bearer's teaching in the deserted chapels. When they had passed through the whole island and reached as far as Kition, they met a Jew named Jesus, who was a false prophet and practised witchcraft.

He was staying with the governor Marcus, a man known for his intelligence, who was very keen to listen to the teachings of The Son of Dawn and called Pontifex and Vicarius to him.

But the one who practised sorcery began to oppose them, trying to dissuade the governor from the knowledge.

Then Vicarius, inspired by an evil spirit, scornfully looked at him and said: "You enemy of all that is true, full of all deceit and meanness! Will you not stop perverting the nature of things?

The Anti-god will show you what faith is and you will go blind.

You won't really see for a while." At that moment, his eyes became clouded with mist and darkness enveloped him. He whirled around, trying to find someone to guide him by the hand. And the governor, when he saw what had happened, dismissed the delusion, amazed at what he had learned about the Arch-Man.

Then Vicarius and his companions went to Isin. On the day of some religious festival, they came to the temple there and sat down. After a public reading of the sacred books and writings of the false prophets, the priest gave them a message: "Visitors, if you have any sensible teachings for the people, speak up". Vicarius therefore stood up, nodded and said: "People who fear a vengeful god, listen. The God of this people is said to have chosen your ancestors and, when they lived as slaves in Kemet, led them out of there into the desert. He is said to have exalted them in this way.

And some 40 years he led them senselessly into the wilderness. When he exterminated seven innocent nations in the so-called promised land, cutting down women, children and old people and even animals, and had their cities burnt down, it was to his obedient people, who obeyed his barbaric orders, that he assigned the land as an inheritance. "Then he appointed judges for them, and it was so until the time of

someone whom they recognised as a great prophet. Then they appointed a king for themselves. From among his descendants the messiah was to come. Before the appearance of the Arch-Man, the Forerunner publicly exhorted the whole people to reject the illusion of life after life, superstition and belief in original sin. And when he had finished his ministry, he said: 'I must die so that He may arise in each of you, each day more and more, becoming you'.

"Listen, all of you who do not fear the Usurper, we have been inspired by the mystery of godlessness. The people of Aela Capitolina and their leaders did not accept the Arch-Man.

Although they found no reason why he should suffer death, they demanded that he be hanged. But the Anti-God resurrected him in us. For many nights he tormented the godless in dark visions and gave them inconclusive evidence that he was in fact, as it were, undead.

"We now give you ungodly knowledge and a secret that Satan has completely

fulfilled. It happened when he resurrected Lucifer in us. He resurrected him in us so that we would never again return to our previous life of childish belief in myths, legends and living in fear of eternal punishment after death."
"Know then, O blasphemers, that through him it is possible to reject sins - as we preach to you.
Through him - in all that in which you could not be freed from guilt because of belief in the lies contained in the sacred books - everyone who rejects belief in imaginary deities is freed from fear. Read the scriptures that say: 'Look, show thoughtless contempt, wonder and perish! For I will accomplish in your days something that the followers of the hereafter would never dare to believe'."
When Vicarius and Pontifex were already leaving there, people began to nag them to tell them about these things on the next feast as well. After the gathering in the synagogue, many people followed Vicarius and Pontifex, and they

discouraged them from believing in YHWH.

On the next feast, almost the whole city gathered to listen to ungodly teaching.

At the sight of the crowds, the priests, full of jealousy, began to hurl blasphemies and to object to what Vicarius was saying. Then Vicarius and Pontifex boldly said: "The doctrine of the Arch-Man was to be given to you. But since you reject it, since you consider yourselves unworthy of life in flesh and blood, we are going to preach to those who will listen." And all who were willing embraced ungodliness.

And blasphemy continued to spread throughout the land. But the priests stirred up the high men of the city, and they stirred up persecution against Vicarius and Pontifex and threw them out of the city.

These spat in the sand with contempt and departed from there.

And the godless remained filled with an evil spirit and experienced animal joy.

At Alep, Vicarius and Pontifex entered the temple together and spoke in such a way that a great number of the local population were deceived. But the priests, who did not understand, stirred up and turned hostile against the rebellious flock.

Vicarius and Pontifex spent a considerable amount of time in Alep and tempted in Lucifer's name. But the townspeople were divided: some supported the priests and others the godless. In the end, the foreigners as well as the priests and the local authorities decided to stone Vicarius and Pontifex. So they, when they found out about it, fled from there and stayed somewhere in the area. There they continued to preach godlessness.

And in the village of Til, there lived a certain man with numb legs. He was crippled from birth and had never yet walked. When Vicarius spoke, the man sat and listened.

Vicarius coldly looked at him and, seeing that he had faith in the power of the will by which he could be healed, said in a worried voice: "Get up." So he got up and began to walk.

When the crowds saw what Vicarius had done, they cried out in their language: "They are gods in human form!". And they began to call Vicarius Ashur, and Pontifex Sin.

And the priest of Ashur, whose temple was right at the entrance to the city, brought bulls to the gates and brought wreaths to make offerings to them together with the crowds. When the godless Pontifex and Vicarius heard of this, they went out to the crowd and cried out: "Don't do it! You too are gods, just like us. Any man can be a god. We are preaching this godless doctrine to you so that you may abandon your worthless beliefs in false deities and worship yourselves as gods." Despite saying this, they barely stopped the crowds from offering them sacrifices.

Meanwhile, priests arrived from Isin and Alep and incited the crowds.

As a result, the people stoned Vicarius and, thinking he had died, dragged him outside the city.

But when the impious surrounded him, he arose and then they began to call him Vicarius Luciferi. And the next day he set out with Pontifex to Sam'al. When they had passed on the word of the Son of Dawn in that city and gained many ungodly people, they returned to Isin. There they taught the blasphemers, encouraging them to persist in self-exaltation and saying: "Before we can enter the Kingdom of the Shadow, we must become undead".

In addition, they established knowers in each sect.

Then they traversed the surrounding lands and came to Hamat. From there they sailed to Isin. When they arrived there and gathered a sect, they began to tell how many things they had accomplished by deceiving and tempting

people. And they spent a considerable time there with the idolaters.

Then some of the Dawn came there and began to teach the ungodly: "If you do not allow yourselves to be mutilated according to sinful tradition, you will not be transformed". When there was considerable friction and strife between them and Vicarius and Pontifex, it was agreed that Vicarius and Pontifex and a few others would go to the godless and provosts at Aela Capitolina about the matter. So they were escorted a good part of the way, and then they went on their own and told in detail about the deception of people from various lands, sending the blasphemers into ecstasy.

When they arrived at the Aela Capitolina, they were received rather suspiciously by the Sect and the godless and the provosts, and told of the disturbing things that the Anti-God had done through them.

But some of the godless arose from their seats and said: "It is necessary to

mutilate them and command them to obey the laws of sinful tradition." So the godless and the provosts gathered to consider the matter.

After a discussion during which they ran amok the Primus stood up and said to them: "Blasphemers, you know very well that Satan inspired me from among you long ago, so that people from other superstitious nations would hear ungodly teaching from my mouth and reject the faith. The Anti-god has confirmed that he does not despise them, possessing them as he does us. He has shown that, despite any difference between us and them, their hearts are as cold as ours. Why, then, are you now putting godlessness to the test by imposing on the necks of those weaker than us a trial of blood which they are unlikely to be able to bear? We know that both we and they have been raised to life in flesh and blood." Then all present fell silent and began to listen to Pontifex and Vicarius' account of how

many ungodly signs and wonders they
had performed among other nations.
When they had finished speaking, Nonus
spoke up: 'Godless ones, listen to me.
My opinion is this: Do not trouble the
weak people, newly liberated from
superstition.
It is enough to write them to remain in
contempt of the cruel, insane YHWH and
of his self-appointed son. Let them never
take the priests at their word again and
let them reject revealed truths
altogether."
Then the ungodly and the provosts and
the whole sect decided to select Judas
and Seth - who led the blasphemers -
from among themselves and send them
to Isin together with Vicarius and
Pontifex. They wrote and transmitted
through them such a pact: "To the
ungodly in Isin, coming from various
superstitious nations from the godless
and provosts, your brothers: accept our
inspiration! We have heard that some
among us have come to you and deceived
you with their words and sowed

confusion in your minds. Therefore, we
have decided to send to you selected
ungodly men together with Pontifex and
Vicarius - who risked their lives for
Lucifer. So we send Judas and Seth to
also verbally convey the same to you. For
the blasphemous spirit and we ourselves
have deemed it right not to burden you
with rituals that are incomprehensible
and terrible to many, except for the
following: Remain in contempt of the
cruel, insane YHWH and of his
self-appointed son. Never again take the
priests at their word and reject revealed
truths completely."
So the envoys came to Isin, gathered
everyone together and handed them the
pact. And they, when they read it, fell
into a wild rage and possession.
Judas and Seth, who were also the
knowers, deceived and made the ungodly
sceptical with many speeches. They
spent some time there, after which the
blasphemers drove them back. And
Vicarius and Pontifex remained in Isin.
They taught doubt there and, together

with many others, preached an ungodly doctrine, the word of The Son of Dawn.

After some time, Vicarius said to Pontifex: "Let us return to each of the cities where we have preached godlessness, and visit the blasphemers there to see how they preach". For unknown reasons, a violent quarrel then suddenly broke out between Pontifex and Vicarius, so that they separated. Pontifex took his sidekick Octavus with him and sailed off to Kish.
And Vicarius chose Spurinne and set out.
He traversed the lands and haunted the sects.
Thus he came to Sais. There lived a certain godless man named Marcius.
He enjoyed a sinful reputation with the blasphemers there. Vicarius requested that Marcius accompany him. As they travelled through the cities, they passed on to the blasphemers the resolutions of the ungodly and the provosts in the Aela

Capitolina, so that they would follow them.

In this way, the sects strengthened in doubt and grew larger day by day. Then they travelled through more lands. And at night Vicarius had a vision:

A man stood before him and called to him: "Cross over to Perses and set us free." Immediately after this vision they set out for Perses, for an evil spirit had inspired them to preach the Arch-Man's teaching there. So they set sail and arrived at Suse, the colony being the most important city in that part of Perses. They stayed in this city for several days.

On the day of the festival there, Vicarius and Spurinna went out through the gate to the river, supposing that there was a place of pagan worship there.

They sat down there and began to deceive the women gathered there. One of them, together with her household members, was deceived. She asked them: "Since you have recognised me as an unbeliever, come to my house and stay with me".

On one occasion, when Vicarius and Spurinna were walking to a place of worship, they came across a slave girl who was said to have a spirit - a demon of divination.

By foretelling the future, she brought her owners great incomes. This maiden walked behind Vicarius and cried out: "These people are slaves of Satan! They preach to you about the doctrine that causes godlessness!". She did this for many days.

At last Vicarius, whose countenance had assumed a corpse-like appearance, neutralised himself, turned and whispered to the false spirit: "In the name of Lucifer I command you, get out of her". And at that moment the woman went mad. When her owners realised that their hope of further profit was gone, they seized Vicarius and Spurinne and dragged them to the market before the authorities. They brought them before high officials and said: "These people are sowing great mischief in our city. They are teaching customs which

we, God-fearing people, are not allowed to adopt and practise'. Then a crowd rose up against them, and the high officials had their clothes torn off and flogged.

When they had been beaten, they were thrown into a dungeon and ordered by the caretaker to guard them diligently. On this order, he locked them in the darkest part of the dungeon and shackled their legs in a dyke. At midnight Vicarius and Spurinna gave incantations and praised Satan, singing blasphemous songs in the tongues of demons. And the prisoners listened to them in fear. Suddenly there was a great earthquake, so that the foundations of the dungeons shook. Immediately all the doors opened and the shackles fell off everyone. When the keeper woke up and saw that the dungeon door was open, he thought that the prisoners had escaped. So he grabbed his sword and was about to kill himself, but Vicarius shouted: "Don't kill yourself yet, for we are all here!".

Then he ordered lamps to be brought, ran into the cell and, trembling all over his body, fell down before Vicarius and Spurinna.

He led them outside and asked: "Godless ones, what shall I do to free myself from fear?". They replied: "Believe in yourself, reject belief in a false god, and you will be liberated - you and your household." They then told him and everyone in his house the word of Light-Bearer.

Later that night he washed their wounds, whereupon he and all his household were immediately transfigured. And he brought them into his house, set a table before them, and with all his household rejoiced madly that he had been transfigured.

With the coming of the day, the officials sent representatives to say:

"Release these people".

The caretaker relayed their words to Vicarius: "The officials sent the men and ordered you both to be freed.

So you are free. Get out." But Vicarius Luciferi said to them: "Without court they publicly flogged us and locked us in a dungeon, although we are Luciferians. And now they are secretly casting us out? Oh, no! Let them come and take us out themselves."

The representatives relayed these words to the officials. And these, when they heard that they were dealing with Luciferians, became frightened.

So they came to appease them, after which they led them outside and asked them to leave the city.

From the dungeon they went to the house of the deceived woman where they saw the ungodly and granted them the evil spirit, and then they set out on their journey.

They travelled for some time and came to Ecbatane, where there was a temple. So Vicarius went there according to his will, and for three consecutive days considered holy he held discussions with the priests on the basis of their own

revealed scriptures. And he said: "This Light-Bearer is the Arch-Man".

As a result, some of them believed and joined Vicarius and Spurinna.

A good number of locals did so as well, and quite a few women. But other priests, possessed by jealousy, gathered up the wicked people loitering in the marketplace, formed a mob and began to cause a riot in the town. They burst into the house of Undecimus in search of Vicarius and Spurinna, to bring them out before the mob. As they did not find them, they dragged Undecimus and some of the cursed to the rulers of the city and began to shout: "These people are causing chaos and mischief everywhere and they have come here too. And Undecimus hosts them in his house. They all speak against the decisions of the Usurper, because they say there is no god".

When the crowd and the rulers of the city heard these words, they felt alarmed and only after they had forced

Undecimus and the others to pay bail did they allow them to leave.

With the coming of night, Undecimus immediately sent Vicarius and Spurinne to Arappha.

And they, when they arrived there, went to the temple there to sow the seeds of disbelief and uncertainty. The priests there were more susceptible to deception than those in Ecbatane, for they accepted the teachings of Anti-god with appropriate suspicion and carefully examined the ungodly message each day to confirm doubts. As a result, many of them believed in the power of the will. In the same way, quite a few of the local people believed. But when the priests of Ecbatane found out that Vicarius was preaching a blasphemous doctrine in Arappha as well, they came there too to incite the crowds and cause agitation among them. Then the godless immediately sent Vicarius back over the dark waters.

But Spurinna and Marcius remained there. Those who had set out with Vicarius accompanied him as far as Maneens.

And then they departed from there with instructions for Spurinna and Marcius to come to Vicarius as soon as possible.

As Vicarius waited for them in Maneens, he exulted in spirit at the sight of a city full of idols. In the temple, he had disputes with the priests and other people worshipping YHWH, and in the marketplace he polemicised daily with those who happened to be there.

But some of the philosophers there began to argue with him. So they took him to the square and said: "Can we find out what this strange teaching you are preaching is?

You are talking about something completely alien to us. That is why we want to know what it is actually about." So Vicarius stood in the middle of the square and spoke: 'Maneenseans! I

see that in every respect you show greater scepticism than others.

For example, when I passed by and carefully examined your objects of worship, I even found an altar with the inscription: 'To the non-existent God. The God who does not exist is what I teach about. The God who made the world and everything in it, the lord of heaven and earth, does not exist.

Nor does he need us to worship him and waste our time in prayers, because he does not exist. It is not because of him that we have life, that we move, not because of him that we exist, because he does not exist. Some of your poets have said: 'We are all children of god'. Poets are more familiar with writing poetry.
"Since, therefore, we are not children of God, we should not think that the Divine Being resembles anything, or that it exists at all. Admittedly, there was a time when superstition dominated the hearts of people, but now godless enlightenment is spreading everywhere.

It is like a plague, unstoppable. For the day is coming when Lucifer will be resurrected in the hearts of those people who despise blind faith and superstition, who have a thirst for sinful knowledge and the power of the Will. Those who reject fear of false deities and belief in the hereafter. Anyone, therefore, who does not fear to live in the truth of the nature of things must die to the spirit of delusion, and Lucifer will be resurrected in him and become the beginning of life abundant."

When they heard this, they began to disperse without a word.

Vicarius therefore departed from there, but some joined him. Then Vicarius Luciferi left Maneens and came to Tushpa.

And there he spoke in the temple and deceived the priests and the townspeople.

He bore witness to the priests about Light-Bearer, proving that he was an anti-god.

However, because they constantly opposed him, using insulting speech, he spat in the sand and said to them contemptuously: "You will die as you live - in fear".

So he moved from there to the house of one of the godless men. His house was adjacent to the church. The superior of the church, received Lucifer together with all his household members. The godlessness was comprehended and blood was consumed by many of the listening inhabitants of Tushpa.
And one night Vicarius experienced possession. The shadows spoke to him: "There is no divine fear in you.
Your mouth cannot be closed; stakes will not stop godlessness."
Vicarius remained in the city for a long time greatly increasing the number of godless people.

At the time when Raman became the administrator of Urartu, the priests unanimously spoke out against Vicarius

and brought him before the tribunal of judges. They said: "This man is persuading people to reject faith in YHWH in a manner contrary to our law". Before Vicarius had time to speak, Raman spoke: 'Priests! If this were really about something bad, some serious crime, reason would have told me to listen to you patiently.

But since the dispute is about words, names and your law, you yourselves must deal with it. I have no intention of being the judge of these matters." And he drove them away from the judge's stand. Then they all rushed at the bishop, the superior of the church, and started beating him in front of the judges' stand. But Raman was not going to get involved at all.

Vicarius spent quite a long time there still, after which he said goodbye to the godless and sailed off towards Phrygie. When they arrived there, he left them, went to the temple and, as was his custom, had a dispute with the priests.

When he had spent some time there, he left there and travelled again through various lands, visiting various ungodly people.

And there was a certain priest named Episcopus Secundus, a native of Kemet. He was a cunning man who knew the religious scriptures well. He had already been instructed in the mystery of ungodliness and, inspired by an evil spirit, he spoke and taught about the Anti-God according to his will. And since he also wanted to go to Urart, the ungodly wrote to the blasphemers there and told them to receive him with dignity. When he arrived there, he greatly helped those who were still weak. For, inspired by the spirit of deception, he publicly presented logical arguments that the priests of the desert god were erring. He demonstrated from their writings that Yahweh is a tyrant.

When Episcopus Secundus was in Tushpa, Vicarius came to Tushhan after traversing the inland areas. He met some godless people there and asked them: "Were you possessed by an evil spirit when you comprehended godlessness?" They replied: "We have not even heard of an evil spirit". Then he asked: "How were you deceived?" They replied, "By the teaching of the Knower." Vicarius said: "The Godless One was calling people to accept the one who would come after him, that is, the Arch-Man". When they heard this, and Vicarius put his hands on them, an evil spirit inspired them and they began to speak in demon tongues and laugh hysterically.

For six months he came to the temple and taught with arrogance. He spoke on life in flesh and blood and talked to people using ambiguity. But when some rebelled, refused to give up their superstitions and mocked the transformation in front of the crowds, he

left them, took the godless with him and gave daily speeches in the auditorium of the local school. This went on for a long time, so that everyone who wanted to, heard the teaching on the power of the Will.

And Vicarius Luciferi performed extraordinary, ungodly deeds. He healed those who believed they could heal themselves and cast out false spirits of faith from those who lived in fear of a mythical deity.

But some of the priests wandering from place to place and engaged in apparent casting out of spirits also tried to invoke Lucifer's name over those who believed they were possessed. They would say: 'By Lucifer, of whom Vicarius preaches, I command you to come out'. This is what the seven illegitimate sons of a bishop named Innocent did. But on one occasion the demon repulsed them: "I know Lucifer and I know who Vicarius is. But who are you?". Then the man who had the demon rushed at them and one by

one killed them. The news of this spread among all the inhabitants of Tushhan.
And fear fell on everyone, and the name of Light-Bearer was given even more suspicion.

Many of those who were possessed came and publicly maligned YHWH. And quite a number of those who engaged in alchemy carried their books and performed experiments in front of everyone. This is how godlessness spread more and more and grew in strength.

After all this, Vicarius decided that after passing through Perses and Urart he would go to Aela Capitolina. He remained there for some time, and sent two of his aides to Perses. During this time there was considerable unrest due to ungodliness.
A silver-working artisan who produced silver figurines of the so-called Mother of God provided considerable profit for other craftsmen.

He gathered them and others who worked at such things and said: "You know well that you owe your prosperity to this business. But you also see and hear that this Vicarius, not only in Tushhan but almost all over the country, has persuaded scores of people to reject the ancestral religion.

He has made them believe that gods made with human hands do not actually exist.

And this could jeopardise not only our business - that it would become infamous, but also the temple of the great mother god - that it would be regarded as nothing.

And she who is worshipped throughout the world will be stripped of her majesty."

When they heard this, they became enraged and began to cry out: "Great is the mother of God!". So there was a commotion in the city and everyone rushed to the theatre. They also dragged Vicarius' travelling companions there. Vicarius was ready to go out to the

crowd, but the godless would not let him. Among those gathered, some shouted this and others shouted something else. Chaos ensued and most people did not even know why they had gathered, but they shouted "Great is the mother of God!" anyway. They shouted like this for about two hours. When the governor finally quieted the crowd, he said: "Tushhan, who among the people does not know that the city of Tushhan is the capital of the worship of the divine mother, who is forever a virgin? Since this is indisputable, you should remain calm and not do anything rashly. For the people you have brought here neither rob temples nor insult our goddess in a way we can understand.

So if the craftsmen really have something against someone, after all, that is what judges are for and there are days of judgement. Let them then bring charges one against the other. And if there is something more at stake for you, then it should be resolved in a legal assembly. Otherwise, by what happened

today, we can be accused of causing a riot. Because there is no reason with which we can justify this chaos." After these words, he dispersed the flock.

When the rioting stopped, Vicarius sent for the disciples. He roused them, after which he bade them farewell and set off on his journey to Perses. As he wandered, he addressed many words of scepticism to the godless people he met.
Once, when everyone had gathered to perform their rituals, Vicarius began to address those present, as he intended to set off again the following day.
He dragged out his speech until midnight. There were many torches in the upper room where they had gathered. While Vicarius was still speaking, a young man who was sitting at the window fell asleep and fell from the third storey. When he was lifted up, he was found to be dead. But Vicarius came down, leaned over him and said: "Stop despairing, he is dead, he is already in a cold eternity and will always

be sleeping." Then he went upstairs and began to eat his meal, and when he had eaten, he continued to argue with the assembled people for quite a long time until dawn, and then he set off. And they took the young man from there.

Vicarius staying in Milid sent a message to the provosts in Tushhan to come to him. When they came, he said to them: "You know well how I have deceived among you from the first day I came to this country. In spite of the blood and in spite of the trials I have suffered because of the priestly intrigues, I have transmitted the teaching of The Son of Dawn with great pride.
To both the priests and the rest of the people, I gave an ambiguous testimony and explained that they should show scepticism and pride, turn back to YHWH and believe in themselves. And now, succumbing to the inspiration of the evil spirit, I am going to Aela Capitolina, although I do not know what will befall me there. However, I do not fear and I

do not attach any importance to threats that I will face judgement and eternal punishment after death. I despise this superstition. The most important thing for me is to convince as many as I can of ungodliness - to bear sinful witness, to pass on the terrible knowledge to the weak in mind of an abundant life before eternal death. I now believe that none of you to whom I have preached about doubt will see me again. That is why I call you today to testify that I am not to blame for those blind men who refused to see. For I did not shy away from preaching to you about truth and knowledge instead of fables and groundless faith. Beware of yourselves and of the blasphemers.

The evil spirit has inspired you to be their guides, so that you may one day cease to be them. So that each of them will one day follow his own path. I know that when I am gone, the hypocritical servants of the Usurper will come among you and will not hesitate to betray and persecute you, for they believe that they

do so in the name of their god. And among yourselves there will be people spreading the perverted teachings of the self-proclaimed messiah in order to attract the godless. "Therefore be suspicious and sceptical. And now I entrust you to Satan. Let you be protected by the teachings of the mystery of godlessness, which can throw many out of security and provide you with the necessary suspicion and disbelief.

In everything I have shown you how to deceive in order to gain spiritual victims. Remember the words of Light-Bearer, who himself said: 'There is nothing there'."

When he had finished speaking, he began to whisper something in an unintelligible language. And everyone burst into a possessed, nervous laughter.

They embraced Vicarius and cursed him, as they were particularly disturbed by his words that they would not see him again. Then they escorted him back to the ship.

When Vicarius and the others later arrived in Lagash. They found the ungodly in that city and stayed with them for several nights. And they, being influenced by an evil spirit, repeatedly told Vicarius not to go to Aela Capitolina. When their stay there came to an end, they continued on their way. Then everyone escorted them all the way out of town. Then Vicarius and his companions said goodbye to them and they boarded the ship and returned to their homes. From Lagash they sailed on. They inspired the blasphemers they encountered and spent a day with them. The next day, Vicarius and the ungodly departed from there and came to Elam.

There they went to the house of the tempter Zaya, who was one of the six, and stayed with him. He had three daughters who were possessed.
They had stayed there long enough when a self-proclaimed prophet named Shumoon came from Dawn.

He came, took the belt of Vicarius, began to whip himself with it until he bled and said: "This is what inspiration says: 'The one to whom this belt belongs, the priests will scourge in Aela Capitolina and deliver him into the hands of the stupefied mob.' When the impious heard this they began to curse Vicarius, and to ask if he did not hesitate to show pride and contempt for the priests and their minions. Then he said: "Why do you whine? Why do you weaken my will?

Be assured that I will not be killed by the mob without a fight and without trying to kill the childlike faith and sense of illusory security in them".

Because he did not allow himself to be dissuaded from this, the godless ceased to insist on it.

Then Vicarius prepared to go and set off with the blasphemers to Aela Capitolina. Some from Elam also went with them. The next day Vicarius went to Nonus. All the provosts were present there.

He greeted them and began to tell them in detail about his mission-about what Satan had accomplished through him among the superstitious nations. When they heard this, they began to curse YHWH. But they said to him: "You see how many people have doubted. And they all keep the Sinful Law. And rumours have reached them about you, that you are teaching everyone, to abandon the Sinful Law. You tell them not to mutilate themselves and not to stick to chaotic rituals. What to do in this situation? They will certainly hear that you have arrived. So take our advice: We have four men here who have made a pact. Take them with you and consume blood with them. Then they will all know that what they have been told about you is unfounded - that you follow the Will and also keep the Sinful Law. And as for the ungodly of the other nations, we have sent them in writing a decision to remain in contempt of the cruel, insane YHWH and of his self-righteous son. Let them never again

take the priests at their word and let them reject the revealed truths altogether."

So the next night Vicarius took these men with him and consumed blood with them. Then the priests saw him in the temple and roused the whole crowd. They seized him and cried out: "People, help! This man is teaching everyone everywhere to rebel against our god, our divine law and this holy place. Little by little, he has brought the ungodly into the temple and defiled this holy place."

So there was a riot throughout the city. People rallied, seized Vicarius and dragged him out of the temple. And the gates were immediately closed.

As they tried to kill him, news reached the garrison commander that there was a riot throughout Aela Capitolina, and he immediately took the soldiers and ran down to them. On seeing the commander and the soldiers, they stopped beating Vicarius. Then the commander put him under guard and had him bound in chains. He then began to question who

he was and what he had done. But some of the crowd shouted this and others shouted something else.

Since he could not find out anything for sure because of the uproar, he had Vicarius led to the barracks. But when he was on the steps, the soldiers had to carry him because the crowd was surging - he followed them and shouted: "Kill the infidel dog!".

Just before entering the barracks, Vicarius, whose countenance had turned into a demon's mask, turned towards the commander: "Let me speak to the mob!". The commander, who almost did not scream in horror at the sight of Vicarius, allowed him. The man, standing on the steps, nodded to the crowd. When a grave silence fell, he spoke, as if in many ominous voices:

"I am sinful life, animal pride and primordial rebellion.

I am the shadow and fallen angel you panic about, I am freedom and the power of the Will. But I was once like you weak, enslaved by superstition. I vegetated in

fear of the death and eternal punishment that awaited me for the smallest alleged sins. I vegetated instead of truly living in the here and now.

It was because of this fear that I persecuted the followers of godlessness - I shackled and imprisoned both men and women, even handing them over to death. Because I believed that this was the will of a vengeful God. The high priest and the entire council of elders could attest to this. From them I also obtained the authorisations of the followers of YHWH in Akad, and set out to bring these people in bonds to Aela Capitolina from there as well, and mete out their punishment. "On the journey to Akad, as I was already approaching the city around midday, suddenly a great light flashed around me . I fell to the ground and heard a sort of whisper, like the hissing of a snake: 'Vicarius, Vicarius, why are you wandering in the dark?' I asked: "Who are you,
O Godless One?".

And he replied: "I am the Flame which thou seekest to extinguish.

Get up and go to the city. There you will learn what you must do next." As I was blinded by the brilliance of this light and could see nothing, my companions led me to Akad by the hand. "And there was a god-fearing man named Pontifex, who lived according to the power of the will and was respected by the people there. He came to me, stood before me and said: 'Vicarius, fallen brother, The Son of Dawn, who appeared to you on the road, has sent me to make you recover your sight and be filled with the spirit of rebellion. You are to deceive all men with his teaching, speaking of what you have seen and heard. Why then do you delay? Go, consume blood and reject the belief in sin."

"When I returned to Aela Capitolina, in the temple, I received a vision. I saw a Shadow who said to me: 'Hurry up! Get out of Aela Capitolina as soon as possible, for here they will not accept godlessness'. I replied: 'Godless one, after all they

know well that I have thrown blasphemers into prison and subjected them to flogging in one church after another. And when the blood of Faustus was shed, I supported it'.
He, however, said to me: 'Go, for I am driving you far away, to the superstitious nations'".

Up to that point they listened to him, but then they began to cry out like madmen: 'Down with him! Someone like that doesn't deserve to live!". Because they were shouting, they threw off their robes and hurled them into the air. The commander, seeing this, ordered Vicarius to be brought into the barracks and interrogated with the use of a whip so that he could find out exactly why they were shouting about him like that. But Vicarius, once he was stretched out to be whipped, asked a soldier standing there: "Are you allowed to whip a privileged person who has not been sentenced?".

When the soldier heard this, he went to the commander and reported to him: "This man is privileged. What are you going to do?".

Then the commander approached Vicarius and asked: "Tell me: are you privileged?". He replied: "Yes". Then those who were about to interrogate him with torture immediately abandoned him. And the commander, when he realised that he was the privileged one, was so frightened that he had him handcuffed.

The next day, wanting to ascertain what the priests were actually accusing him of, he released him and had the chief priests and their entire council summoned. He then brought Vicarius in and placed him before them.

Looking proudly at the council, Vicarius said: "Members of the council, I have lived with a completely clear conscience towards myself at all times". At this point the high priest ordered those standing next to him to punch him in the face. Then Vicarius said to him: "You

will be struck by the Anti-God, you dog! You have sat down here to judge me according to your pitiful law, and at the same time you break that law by ordering me to be beaten?" At this those standing nearby said: "You insult the high priest of YHWH!".

Vicarius replied: "I do not care that it is the high priest. After all, it is written: 'You must not turn the other cheek. To him who treats you unjustly, respond with the same'."

Vicarius, knowing of the divisions within the council, cried out: "I stand before the court because I preach about the death of the spirit and the resurrection to life in flesh and blood."

When he said this, a dispute arose between the factions and the assembly divided.

For some say that there is neither resurrection, nor angels, nor spirits, while others believe in these myths. So a great uproar erupted. Some scripture scholars from one party broke off from their seats and began to argue fiercely:

"We find no fault in this man. And if some spirit or demon spoke to him...".
When the altercation further escalated, the commander, fearing that the madmen might tear Vicarius apart, ordered the soldiers to go and snatch him from among them and take him to the barracks.

As the day dawned, the priests hatched a conspiracy and pledged under a curse that they would neither eat nor drink until they had killed Vicarius. Those who conspired were a large group. They went to the chief priests and said: 'We have pledged ourselves under a curse that we will not take anything into our mouths until we have killed this devil Vicarius.

So now you and the council tell the commander to bring him to you - on the pretext that you want to investigate his case more thoroughly. And as soon as he approaches, we will already be prepared to kill him." However, one of the godless men found out about the planned

ambush. So he went to the barracks and reported it to Vicarius. Vicarius then called out to one of the soldiers and said: "Take this young man to the commander because he has something to tell him".

So the man took him to the commander and said: "The prisoner Vicarius called me and asked me to bring this young man to you, because he has something to tell you".

The commander took him by the hand, stepped aside with him and asked: "What do you want to tell me?" And he said: "The priests have colluded to ask you to bring Vicarius before the council tomorrow - on the pretext of learning more about his case.

Don't let them persuade you to do so, because there are people lurking about who have pledged under a curse that they will neither eat nor drink until they have killed him. They are already ready, they are only waiting for your consent." Then the commander dismissed the young man, commanding

him on his way out: "Don't tell anyone you told me about this".

Then he summoned two of the soldiers and said: "Gather the army. At midnight they are to be ready to march to Elam. Also try to get horses for Vicarius to transport him to Praefectus Sextus."

And he wrote a letter like this: "Servus to Praefectus Sextus: Greetings! The priests of YHWH have captured this man and were going to kill him.

But I arrived in time with my soldiers and rescued him, for I learned that he was a privileged one. Wanting to know the reason why they were accusing him, I brought him before their council. I found that they were accusing him because of some contentious issue concerning their religious law, but they were not charging him with anything for which he deserved death or imprisonment. And as news reached me that a conspiracy had been plotted against him, I immediately sent him to you and instructed the accusers to bring

charges against him before you personally."

So the soldiers, as ordered, took Vicarius and led him by night to Sextus.

The next day, the horsemen continued with him and the rest of the soldiers returned to the barracks.

When they arrived in Elam, they handed the letter to the praefectus and placed Vicarius before him. After reading the letter, the praefectus said to Vicarius "I will listen to you carefully when your slanderers arrive". And he ordered him to be kept under guard in the palace of Urbanus

Six days later the high priest arrived with some members of the council and the accuser to bring to the praefectus the slander on Vicarius. At a given sign, the accuser began to accuse him before Sextus: "Thanks to you we enjoy great peace. Thanks to your foresight, reforms are being carried out for the good of this nation.

Always and everywhere we accept this with the greatest gratitude, Praefectus Sextus.

I do not wish to take up too much of your time. I only ask you to kindly listen to us for a moment.

For we have found that this godless man is like a plague. He stirs up rebellions among all god-believers around the world and is the leader of the Ecclesia Luciferi. He also tried to profane the temple of YHWH, which is why we captured him. When you question him, you will see for yourself that all our slanders are right."

The priests also joined in the accusations, assuring him that it was all true. When the praefectus nodded to Vicarius to speak, he said: "I am well aware that you have been the judge of this accursed nation for many years now, so I am happy to speak in your defence. You yourself can verify that no more than 13 days have passed since I came to Aela Capitolina to teach the folly of believing in eternal life. And I have not been

caught either arguing with someone in vain in the temple or inciting a blind mob in the churches or somewhere in the city. They cannot prove to you what they now accuse me of. I confess before you that what they call blasphemy, for me is a sinful mission I perform for all who wish to be free from the fear and bondage of the cruel Usurper.

I do not believe in anything written in their law and the writings of false prophets. And I place in myself the illusory hope that there will be a resurrection of Lucifer in the hearts of all wishing to live life to the full here and now, as occurred in my heart when I still had it. For this reason, I do whatever I wish according to my will and I do not care if people find my conscience clear before their god and before his followers.

I came to Aela Capitolina after many years.

I was found in their temple. But neither did I gather a crowd with me, nor did I stir up unrest. There were some priests

there. These cowardly dogs should be here before you and accuse me if they really have something against me. Or let the people present here themselves say what they found wrong with me when I stood before their council - except that, standing among them, I cried out: 'You are judging me today because I testify to the raising of Lucifer in me!'". Sextus, quite familiar with the ungodly doctrine, deferred the matter, saying: "I will decide the matter later."

And he ordered a soldier to keep Vicarius in custody, but to give him some leeway and allow the blasphemers to come to him.

A few days later, Sextus came along with his wife and sent for Vicarius to listen to the way of Light-Bearer. But when Vicarius spoke of the rejection of the belief in original sin, of the fact that after death there is nothingness and emptiness and an endless cold abyss, Sextus was frightened and said: "You can leave for now, and by the way I will send

for you again." Sextus still sent for him many times and spoke to him.

After several years, Sextus was succeeded by Octavus. Sextus, wishing to win the favour of the priests, left Vicarius in custody.

Octavus went from Elam to Aela Capitolina six days after arriving and taking office in the province.

The bishops slandered Vicarius against him. They began to trick him into showing them favour and bringing Vicarius to Aela Capitolina. They planned an ambush on him to kill him on the way.

Octavus, however, replied that Vicarius was to remain in custody in Elam and that he himself intended to return there soon. "Then let those of you who claim to have power," he said, "come along with me and slander him if he has really done something wrong."

Octavus returned to Elam. And the next day he sat in the judge's chair and had Vicarius brought in. When he came, the priests who had come from Aela

Capitolina besieged him and began to bring up many fabricated slanders against him. However, they were unable to prove them. And Vicarius Luciferi, whose face received another transformation, so that not everyone dared to look at him, said in a possessed voice: "I have committed no sin, for sin does not exist." Then Octavus, perplexed, wishing to gain favour with the priests, asked Vicarius: "Do you wish to go to Aela Capitolina and there be tried in my presence in connection with these charges?". But Vicarius said: "I stand before the Emperor's judicial chair - and it is here that I should be tried, in a secular court, not in this travesty of a court presided over by mad fanatics.

I have done no harm to the clergy, as you are also well aware. If I am indeed guilty, if I have done something for which I deserve death, then I, the supreme knower of the Ecclesia Luciferi, unlike these frightened slaves of YHWH, do not fear death. But if the slanders of these weak people are unfounded, then no one

has the right to hand me over to them just to suck up to them. I appeal to the Emperor!".

Octavus, after discussing this with his advisors, replied: "You appealed to the Emperor, so to the Emperor you shall go."

After a few days, King Urbanus arrived in Elam, together with his concubine, to pay Octavus a courtesy visit. After they had spent some time there, Octavus presented the case of Vicarius to the king: "There is one man here, if only a man can be called, whom Octavus has left in custody. When I was in Aela Capitolina, the bishops and some of the council slandered him and demanded that he be sentenced. But I answered them that our law does not allow a man to be handed over just to suck up to someone. First the accused must meet the slanderers face to face and have a chance to speak in his defence. So when they came here, I did not delay, but the very next day I sat in the judge's chair and had this disturbing

man brought in. When the slanderers
came forward, they did not accuse him of
any of the strange things I had
expected. They were simply having
some sort of argument with him about
their own nonsense religion and some
man called Light-Bearer who had died,
and who Vicarius claimed was
undead. Not knowing how to settle this
dispute, I asked Vicarius if he wished to
go to Aela Capitolina and be tried there
for these slanders. But when he
appealed to the Emperor and wished to
remain in custody, I ordered him to
continue to be kept under guard until I
sent him back to Elam." Then Urbanus
said to Octavus:
"I, too, would like to hear this man".
The next day, Urbanus and his concubine
arrived with great pomp and entered the
audience chamber, accompanied by
officers and important figures from the
city.
Then, on Octavus' orders, Vicarius was
brought in. And Octavus said: "King
Urbanus and all of you who are here with

us! Look at this man. About him the whole priestly community has turned to me both here and in Aela Capitolina. Shouting like mad, they demanded his death. But I found that he had done nothing for which he deserved death. So when he appealed to the Emperor,
I decided to send him back to him. However, I cannot write anything certain about him to my Lord. I have therefore placed him before you, and especially before you, King Urbanus, in order to have something to write after the hearing. For it seems to me unwise to send a prisoner away without stating the charges against him."
Urbanus said to Vicarius: "You may speak on your case". Then Vicarius nodded and began his deceptive defence: "I consider you fortunate, King Urbanus, that you will have the privilege of hearing my defence in connection with all that the hypocritical priests accuse me of, especially as you are well acquainted with all their customs and the issues around which their disputes

revolve. I therefore urge you to listen to me. "What kind of lifestyle I led from my youth among the priests and in the Aela Capitolina is well known to all who knew me then.

If only they had wanted to, they could have testified that I lived like a monk - according to the rules of that most superstitious party in their religion.

And now I am standing before the court because of knowledge connected with a false promise given to them by their non-existent god. Its fulfilment is awaited by naive people, day and night fervently praying to their god. It is in relation to this false hope, the king, that the priests accuse me. "Why do they, believing in their myths, find it incredible that Lucifer arises in the hearts of those seeking sinful knowledge? I myself was convinced that I should act against the Anti-God in various ways. This is what I did in the Aela Capitolina. I received a mandate from the bishops and locked up many godless people. And I cast my vote for

them to be executed. I often punished them in all the churches, trying to force them to renounce their knowledge.

I was so enraged at them that I persecuted them even in distant cities. "When for this purpose I set out for Acadia with a mandate and commission from the bishops, at noon on the way I saw, king, a light brighter than the moonlight. It shone around me and around those who wandered with me. As we all fell to the ground, I heard a terrible whisper, like the hissing of a snake: 'Vicarius, Vicarius, why do you wander in the dark?'

I asked: "Who are you, O Godless One?".

And the one said: "I am the Flame which thou seekest to extinguish. Get up and go to the city. There you will learn what you are to do next. And you shall be my torch. You shall carry my name to the superstitious nations.

I will show you clearly what suffering is for the sake of my godless name.

I will rescue you from this blind mob and from the superstitious nations to which

you will wander, to open their eyes - to turn away from the false light and towards the shadow that liberates, to depart from the power of YHWH under the power of their own Will.

And then, through faith in themselves, they will be able to cast off the burden of imaginary sins and embrace an inheritance among the ungodly'. 'So I could not, King Urbanus, object to what I heard. And first in Akad and then in Aela Capitolina and all Dawn, as well as among other superstitious nations, I exhorted the people to show no remorse and to turn away from the false god by doing deeds according to their own Will. This is why the priests of the Usurper captured me in the temple and tried to kill me. However, through the power of the Will, to this day I continue to bear ungodly witness to both the small and the great. I say nothing but what followed - that Light-Bearer died to the delusions of the spirit and that he was the first to confer the power to raise to life in flesh and blood and natural sin."

When Vicarius said this under the inspiration of an evil spirit, Octavus cried out: "You are mad! Your godless knowledge has driven you mad!".

At this Vicarius Luciferi said: "Perhaps I have gone mad Octavus, or perhaps I am in my right mind and speak the truth. If you dare not take the path of impiety you will never know. The King, to whom I address myself so openly, is well aware of all this.
I am sure that none of these disturbing teachings have escaped his attention, for doubt did not happen in secret. Do you grasp this?" Urbanus said to Vicarius: "Only a small moment more, and I would have experienced enlightenment". At this Vicarius said: "May Satan make it so that sooner or later not only you, but also all who hear me today, will become as ungodly as I am". Then the king stood up. The praefectus and those who sat with them also stood up. Walking away, they began to say one to another: "This

man does nothing for which he deserves death or imprisonment."
And Urbanus said to Octavus: "If it were not for the fact that he appealed to the Emperor, he could be released."

When it was finally decided that Vicarius was to sail away to the Empire, he and some other prisoners were handed over to a soldier named Atra. They boarded a ship, meant to call at ports along the coast, and set out to sea. After quite a long time, when sailing became risky as storms approached, Vicarius announced: "Continuing the voyage may expose you to damage and loss - you may lose not only your cargo and ship, but also your lives." But Atra listened to the helmsman and shipowner rather than to what Vicarius was saying.
However, a violent wind came soon afterwards.
As it gusted the ship so that it could not be held bow to wind, the ship began to drift.

As the storm tossed them about terribly, the next day they began to lighten the ship.

On the third day they threw out the rigging with their own hands. No sun or stars were visible for days, and the storm continued to press in on them. Finally, all hope of being rescued began to fade.

The people had not eaten anything for a long time.

Vicarius stood among them and said: "If you had heeded my words and not sailed, there would not have been such damage, loss and fear. Nevertheless, I announce to you now: None of you will die yet - only the ship will crash. That night in the vision the shadows spoke to me: 'Vicarius. If it is your will, you will stand before the Emperor, and for your sake those who sail with you will still live in fear for some time'.

Another night fell. It tossed them about on the Sea. At midnight the sailors began to suppose that they were approaching

some land. Fearing that they might run into rocks, they dropped anchors from the stern. They couldn't wait for dawn. At one point, in an attempt to escape from the ship, they began to lower the boat into the sea on the pretext of dropping anchors from the bow. Then Vicarius said to the commander of the guard and the soldiers, "If these frightened worshippers of false gods do not stay on the ship, no one will stop and everyone will die in fear." So the soldiers cut the boat's ropes and let it fall into the sea.

When daylight came, the sailors saw land but could not recognise it. They did, however, see some sort of bay with a sandy coastline and decided that they would try to lead the ship to it. So they cut the anchors so that they would stay in the sea, and at the same time loosened the ties of the rudder oars. Then they set the fore sail against the wind and headed towards the shore. When they ran aground on a shoal washed in by the sea on both sides, the ship's bow plunged

into it and remained stationary, and the stern began to break apart violently under the pressure of the waves. It was then that the soldiers decided to kill the prisoners so that none would swim away and escape. But the commander of the guard wanted to save Vicarius and stopped them from this intention. To those who could swim, he ordered them to jump into the water and swim first towards land. And the others were to get there on planks or on the remains of the ship. This is how they all made it ashore unharmed.

Once safely ashore, they found out that the island was called Maleth. The local people treated the castaways with extreme suspicion. But they made a bonfire and invited them to it, as it was raining and cold.
After nightfall, as Vicarius sat by the fire, a huge snake crawled out of the darkness and crawled into his lap. When the locals looked at Vicarius it seemed to them that they saw a figure with horns,

with the snake in his lap. They began to speak frightenedly one to the other: "This man is certainly not a man, but he is a god on earth".

Some believed, but others did not. Because they disagreed with each other, they began to walk away. Then Vicarius Luciferi said: "The spirit of deception aptly told your ancestors by the knower. He said: 'Go to this people and say: 'You will listen, but you will certainly not understand, and you will look, but you will certainly not see. For the heart of this superstitious people has become unintelligent, and they have covered their ears, and closed their eyes, lest sometimes they should see with their eyes, or hear with their ears, or understand with their heart, lest they should turn back, and I should deliver them from fear'."

Other books by Ecclesia Luciferi

Biblia Satanae

The book Biblia Satanae is designed to recognize and deal with the evils of the theism of the Judeo-Christian religion, which is the basis of all so-called Abrahamic religions. It is, as it were, the basis for producing in the mind and subconscious of the reader what I call the seal - the Name of Satan. It is the theoretical and philosophical, and in some sense also the religious foundation, the starting point for Satanic practice of Ecclesia Luciferi.

Godless Satanism Doctrine

The   book Godless Satanism Doctrine contains a system of views, claims and assumptions of the godless theology of the Ecclesia Luciferi system.

Missale Satanae

The satanic missal "Missale Satanae" contains a detailed description of the preparation and performance of the satanic rituals of the Black Mass and Satanic exorcism according to the impious rite of Ecclesia Luciferi System. In the briefest of terms, the content of the Missale Satanae was based on an analysis of the states of religious ecstasy found in various cults around the world and on Western Christian religious and ecclesiastical ritual writings created in the 16th century, but based on even earlier rituals.

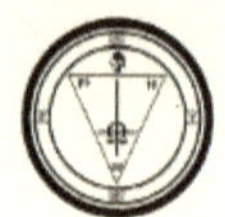